PSYCHO-PHONE MESSAGES

RECORDED BY
FRANCIS GRIERSON

New York

Published by Curious Publications.
curiouspublications.com
Copyright © 2020

First published in 1921 by Austin Publishing Company.

Cover image is pulled from an article that appeared in the *Richmond Times-Dispatch*, October 24, 1920.
Photo of Francis Grierson by Russell & Sons, from the June 1903 issue of *The Critic*.
"A Note on the Text" written by Marc Hartzman.

ISBN-13: 978-0-9862393-7-3

Printed and bound in the United States of America.

A NOTE ON THE TEXT

The book you now hold was originally published in 1921 by Francis Grierson, a mystic, musician, poet, prophet, and overall man of many talents. Grierson was born as Benjamin Henry Jesse Francis Shepard in 1848 in England, but grew up in Illinois. He later took his mother's maiden name when publishing *Modern Mysticism* in 1899. By 1915, the *Washington Herald* hailed Grierson as the "Strangest Man in the World."

"So great, varied and unearthly are Grierson's gifts that it is difficult to consider him as a human being," the paper wrote. "If he had lived in ancient times his contemporaries would have made an oracle, prophet or saint out of him."

His most particular talent was on display at the piano, where he completely improvised without ever learning to read a note of music. Grierson's abilities led him to travels throughout Europe playing before crowned heads and causing Alexandre Dumas to say, "I predict for you a marvelous future."

That future included an interest in Spiritualism. Grierson conducted séances across America and Europe, and in the late 1880s built a home in San Diego called Villa Montezuma. It would become a temple to occultism, with many séances being held within.

This book, Grierson's last, features messages from beyond the veil from a number of luminaries, all of which, he claimed, were recorded through the "psycho-phone." Was this a device? His mind? Or simply more of his improvisational talents on display?

What follows is the book as it appeared in 1921, including the original cover. It's up to you, the reader, to take what you will from it.

PSYCHO-PHONE MESSAGES

RECORDED BY
FRANCIS GRIERSON

Spiritual Messages from the late General U. S. Grant, on Adequate Preparation in America; Thomas Jefferson, on the Future of American Democracy; Benjamin Disraeli, on English and Irish Affairs; Prince Bismarck, on the Indemnities; John Marshall, on the Psychology of the Supreme Court of the United States; Alexander Hamilton, on the Forces that Precede Revolution; Abraham Lincoln, on the Future of Mexico; Robert Ingersoll, on Our Great Women; Henry Ward Beecher, on the New Puritanism; Benjamin Wade, of Ohio, on President Harding; General B. H. Grierson, on Japan, Mexico and California, etc.

PSYCHO-PHONE MESSAGES

RECORDED BY
FRANCIS GRIERSON

Published by
AUSTIN PUBLISHING COMPANY
Los Angeles, California
June, 1921

INTRODUCTION

The word "psycho-phone" was first suggested and used by Mr. Francis Grierson in a lecture I heard him deliver before the Toronto Theosophical Society, August 31st, 1919, a year before Thomas Edison announced his intention of devising an instrument which he hopes will serve to establish intercourse between our world and the world of spirit.

My own experiences as a student in this sphere of psychic research in Europe and America, covering a period of thirty years, convince me that we have here a revelation of a new mode of spiritual communication unlike anything heretofore given to the world, not only different in quality but different in purpose.

From personal knowledge I can state that the recorder of these messages has not acted on ideas advanced by anyone living on our plane.

Looking back over the past two decades, I am led to believe that Mr. Grierson's predictions in "The Invincible Alliance," and in that startling poem, "The Awakening in Westminster Abbey," forecasting the war and the tragic events in Ireland, were spiritual and psycho-phonic in character.

From 1909 to 1911 Francis Grierson was the acknowledged leading writer on "The New Age," of London, which at that time had as contributors, H. G. Wells, Bernard Shaw, Arnold Bennett, the two Chestertons, Hillaire Belloc—in one word, all the most prominent writers and advanced thinkers in Britain, yet not one of them except

Mr. Grierson could see the approaching world upheaval.

Early in 1909 he published a series of articles in that weekly depicting the coming war, and nothing of so drastic a nature had ever appeared in an English publication. In the spring of 1913 these articles were published in book form in London and New York under the title of "The Invincible Alliance."

In the Westminster Abbey composition, published in "The New Age" in 1910, the characteristics of four personalities are plainly manifest—Coleridge, Milton, Shelley and Shakespeare—and I have not forgotten the sensation caused by this great work in London at the time of its appearance.

Having had occasion to study the social and psychic conditions in France, Germany, Italy, Austria and England before the great war, and after having been an eye witness of scenes unique in the annals of musical inspiration in the artistic and literary circles of Europe as well as the most intellectual of the royal courts, in which Mr. Grierson was the central figure, I now have a better understanding of the work he accomplished and its far-reaching import. The more complex the work the longer must be the preparation, and we are now confronted with what will appear to many as the most interesting phase of Mr. Grierson's psychic gifts, for the seer who ushered in the new mystical movement by the publication of "Modern Mysticism" in 1899 is now the recorder of messages which must induce thinking and unprejudiced minds to pause and consider such matters in a new light, and it is to be hoped that many more messages like these may be recorded by the same hand.

As I write, I have before me a unique collection of letters written to Mr. Grierson by men and women eminent in philosophy, art, music, literature and journalism, in Europe and America. Among the letters that Mr. Grierson values the most in this remarkable album are eight from members of the French Academy, with Sully Prudhomme, winner of the first Noble Prize, heading the list. Which reminds me that I heard him say one evening in Paris, after hearing Mr. Grierson's music: "You have placed me on the threshold of the other world. There are not words in the French language to express what I have felt tonight!" Up to that moment the famous Academician had been known as an avowed agnostic.

Maeterlinck writes that the first Grierson volume (in French) influenced him more than any book he had ever read. There are four letters from the Belgian mystic.

This album is filled with expressions from the most authoritative minds in literature and art, as well as statesmen, soldiers and diplomats, such as Jules Simon, the Duc de Broglie, Lord Lytton, British ambassador at Paris; Lord Reading, British ambassador at Washington; Field Marshall Lord Wolseley, General B. H. Grierson, U.S.A., leading members of the Bonaparte family in Paris, Prince Henri of Orleans (son of Louis Philippe), Princess Eulalia of Spain, and crowned heads who gave receptions in Mr. Grierson's honor during the past thirty years. There are letters from distinguished Americans, such as Col. Henry Watterson (who wrote two long editorials on Mr. Grierson in the Louisville "Courier Journal"), Henry Mills Alden, editor of "Harper's Monthly," Prof. William James, Marion Reedy, Edwin Markham, Edith Thomas, Mary Austin, and many leading professors of Harvard, Yale, Columbia, Cornell, the Universities of Illinois, Wisconsin and California.

Edwin Bjorkman says, in his "Voices of Tomorrow":—

"To Francis Grierson belongs the honor of having first attained to prophetic vision of the common goal. In his first volume, published in Paris in 1889, he suggested every idea which since then has become recognized as essential not only to Bergson and Maeterlinck but to the constantly increasing number of writers engaged in making the time conscious of its own spirit. As we read essay after essay it is as if we beheld the globe of life revolving slowly between us and some unknown source of light."

The following remarks from the London "Outlook" seem to me pertinent to the subject:—

"Grierson is an Englishman, for he was born in Cheshire; Scotland may justly claim him in that he is a direct descendent of Sir Robert Grierson, the famous Laird of Lag, who is the hero of Scott's novel, 'The Red Gauntlet'; that America has had a part in the making of him all readers of that wonderful book, 'The Valley of Shadows,' know; France can claim him since he began his musical career in Paris and published his first book in French; but no special country can claim to have developed his genius—that is cosmopolitan."

As "Current Opinion" says, in a long study: "He presents a unique combination of thinker, writer, artist and musician who owes nothing to any school or any master or system of training; and his experience is without a parallel in the intellectual world of our day."

LAWRENCE WALDEMAR TONNER,
245½ So. Spring St.
Los Angeles, California.

FOREWORD

These messages were begun in September, 1920, and the last was recorded in May, 1921. I little dreamed that many of the predictions set forth would be verified so soon. For names, in themselves, count for nothing. The subliminal mind may assume different names on different occasions. A message is of value exactly in proportion to the information imparted.

The first communication from General Grant was recorded September ninth. It is peremptory in tone, and contains a warning touching the insecurity of the Panama Canal. In November Mr. Harding made a tour of inspection and found the fortifications of the Canal inadequate. I then decided on the publication of these messages.

They deal with the actual. Take, for example, John Marshall's documents, which are filled with warnings no reader with intelligence will attempt to refute, Disraeli's indictment of English statesmanship in recent times, Lincoln's utterances on affairs in Europe and Mexico, General Grant on Preparation, Benjamin Franklin on the Privilege of Liberty, Bishop Phillips Brooks on the Coming Ordeals, to name but a few.

As a Judge sums up, regardless of who may or may not agree, a decision is rendered according to the vision of the one who delivers the message. Principle, not Party, is the basis of judgment.

Witness Disraeli's remark that the blunders committed by the British Parliament would have been impossible in an Irish Parliament in Dublin.

In a series of articles in "Nash's Magazine" Mr. Basil King suggests that "the means of communication with the plane next above us may be through the everlasting doors which the subliminal opens upward. Through these doors the mind may go up and out; through these doors the light may come in and down."

In our group of investigators we have had the perseverence essential for serious development, and, as in all demonstrations, whether physical or psychical, everything depends on conditions, so we have had periods of weeks when no message of any kind was received.

A striking feature of these communications is their freedom from restraint imposed by popular opinion. They contain neither theories nor appeals. Warnings are uttered concerning events and their inevitable reactions.

The psycho-phonic waves, by which the messages are imparted, are as definite as those received by wireless methods.

FRANCIS GRIERSON.
Los Angeles, California

CONTENTS

	PAGE
Introduction	11
Foreword	15
Thomas Reed, of Maine, Late Speaker of the House, on the Peace League	21
General U. S. Grant, on Adequate Preparation in America	23
General U. S. Grant (second message)	25
Thomas Jefferson, on the Future of American Democracy	27
Elizabeth Cady Stanton, on the Future of American Women	29
Benjamin Franklin, on the Privilege of Liberty	34
John Marshall, "The Expounder of the Constitution," on the Psychology of the Supreme Court	36
Daniel Webster, on "Bohemian" Statesmen	37
Oliver Wendell Holmes, on the New Eden	38
Benjamin Wade, Late Governor of Ohio, U. S. Senator, on President Harding	39
Don Piatt, Late Editor of "The Capital," Washington, D. C., on Prohibition and the Blue Laws	42
Benjamin Disraeli, on English and Irish Affairs	44
Prince Bismarck, on Germany and the Indemnities	47
Henry Ward Beecher, on the New Puritanism	51

John Marshall, on Liberty and the League
(second message) 53
Abraham Lincoln, on the Future of Mexico 56
Robert Ingersoll, on Our Great Women 58
Stephen A. Douglass, on War Between
England and America 59
General B. H. Grierson, on Japan and California 69
Alexander Hamilton, on the Forces that
Precede Revolution 62
Phillips Brooks, on The Coming Ordeals 64

Psycho-phone Messages

THOMAS B. REED
(Late Speaker of the House)
Recorded September seventh, 1920.

The formidable imbecility of the Senate rivaled the fantastic irritability of the President.

Born with a Utopian temperament, Mr. Wilson has a Herculean passion for generalities and a Lilliputian penchant for details.

You scratched the Teutons at Versailles and found a new species of Tartar; you scratched the Japanese and found a Pacifist camouflage; you scratched the Poles and found a pianist with his hair uncut; you scratched the French and found a tiger with his claws unclipped. Your mania for scratching other nations will keep your nails manicured without the aid of scissors.

Never since the Declaration of Independence and the first peal of the Liberty Bell did a chief executive walk up a winding stair into so pretty a parlor as when Mr. Wilson, with the naivete of a Princeton president, faced that cacophony of sectional jazz bands to witness the cryptic hand-writing on the wall at the peace table. Who was his adviser? Was it a gentleman with owl spectacles from the oil fields of Texas? And was there no one who could have cautioned him against the finesse of Clemenceau who spent sixty years sharpening his wits on the political grindstone of Europe? Was no one in America aware that the French Premier is a fluent speaker in English?

Mr. Wilson could speak no French, which reminds me that Jack

Spratt could eat no fat and his wife could eat no lean, and so betwixt them both they licked the platter clean. But a clean plate does not mean a clean slate, and the President brought one home filled with the riddle of the Sphinx. Yet the Peace Conference revealed the secret of perpetual motion and conferred a timely service, for the hubbub created by the Wilson-Lansing-House-Party at Versailles kept the Senate from passing into a trance.

A blind man can tell the difference between pepper pods and apple dumplings, but who can tell where tweedle-dee ends and tweedle-dum begins? No one. Then how can your statesmen distinguish between the psychological characteristics of the Hungarians and the Bohemians, the Bavarians and the Saxons, the difference between a polka and a polonaise, a pig in a stye and a pig in a slaughter house? Patriotism often depends on an influence too subtle for analysis, and yet they would enact drastic laws to bind all Europe in one bond. They will hardly succeed in a thousand years.

Some pay through the nose, some through the pocket and some through the stomach. Americans are paying through all three. Danton declared the secret of the French Revolution was audacity, and audacity, and again audacity, but what you need today is vigilance repeated ad infinitum.

I am placing you in communication with some of the most far-reaching minds of the past hundred and fifty years. The psycho-phone is new and we are using it for the first time.

THE LATE GENERAL U. S. GRANT
Recorded September Ninth, 1920

The imbroglio started by President Carranza is beginning to influence the politicians of Buenos Ayres and other centers in South America. They have secretly repudiated the Monroe Doctrine. Their next maneuver will be a public repudiation.

I would say to Congress, stop juggling with phrases and attend to the business of the hour. The majority have been chasing shadows in a sphere of politics illumined by moonshine bottled in the Blue Ridge. I was more careful of my brand. When President Lincoln asked for the label, so he could recommend it to other generals, he was not far wrong in his surmises. It is not so much the thing as the quality that counts. Most of you at Washington will have to learn the difference between inhibition and prohibition.

The United States will be isolated within three years from this date if the blowhards from the woolly constituencies are not suppressed. You need a broncho buster in the Senate and a donkey muzzler in the House.

When a boycott is started by the countries south of the Union your enemies in Europe will begin to act. It is not a question of commerce but of common sense. I repeat what Lincoln said in 1862: "The times are dark and the spirits of ruin are abroad in all their power."

My message to Congress is: See that fifty thousand troops are stationed permanently near the District of Columbia.

My message to the Governors of New York, Pennsylvania and Illinois is: Get ready! The troops on the borders of Texas, New Mexico and Arizona are inadequate. The fortifications of the Panama and at San Diego and San Pedro are inadequate. You are in the same condition the French were in previous to 1789, when the motto was, "After us the Deluge." The Deluge came but it did not consist of water.

Our foes of the old Germany and the new Russia count on crippling the United States through South America, with the aid of Japan; but he who delivers the first blow will be the victor.

The Germans still believe they can eventually invade France, enter Paris and cause a revolution, found a new empire to include France, Belgium, Holland and Switzerland, with Italy later on. This dream includes a practical understanding with Soviet Russia, which, by that time, they expect would be weary of futile experiments. Plots will be exposed that will make it apparent how vain some of your optimistic surmises have been. Diplomats who are not psychologists will be balked by developments in Switzerland, that nation having become the rendezvous of disillusioned wire-pullers without a country. You are now at the cross roads. Take the wrong turning and you will come to the skull and cross bones.

I could say much more but we are not yet experts in this new mode of inter-communication and must be brief.

GENERAL U. S. GRANT
(Second Message)
Recorded May Third, 1921

I concur with Alexander Stephens when he says: "Congress has never been so supine and so serpentine."

Millions are sent to the people of distant countries in no way related to our Government or people, and yet Congress permits thousands of veterans of the great war to continue in a state of neglect, suffering and humiliation.

Do the authorities believe that when the day of trial arrives the friends and relatives of these veterans will hurry to volunteer for active service? The country is being fascinated by incidents and events in far-off regions, and the tragic conditions at home have entered a chronic stage.

There are too many old men in Congress—men who never did more than fight grasshoppers or watch a game of football from reserved seats.

We do not like the looks of the President's pronunciamento. It contains too many side issues. He is making Mr. Wilson's mistake of being verbose. Mr. Wilson tried to hypnotize Europe; the Senate is trying to hypnotize Mr. Harding. Popularity breeds as much contempt as familiarity. No President can ever succeed in conciliating all classes, sections and parties.

The politicians of Buenos Ayres have now spoken as I predicted in my first message. They have attacked Mr. Harding for his speech on Pan-Americanism, all which goes to prove that the President is repeating for South America Mr. Wilson's blunders in France.

Remember what Lincoln said to Judge Whitney:—

"Those fellows think I don't see anything, but I see all around them. I see better what they want to do with me than they do themselves."

The politicians of South America see better what the President wants to do with them than he does himself.

The administration will face a critical period in the early fall. There will be a break in the dominant phalanx. A social and political readjustment will compel mediation in quarters the most unexpected.

The new political and commercial dispensation for the English-speaking countries will begin on September twenty-second at two P.M.

THOMAS JEFFERSON

Few politicians understand the difference between scene-shifting and progress. Things shift, new names are applied, but the vicious circle continues.

I see no evidence that human nature has changed since my time, in this or any other country.

If the Republican Ship of State is leaking, the Democratic craft is drifting without sail or rudder. What your statesmen fail to understand is that progress is not induced by force but by free will. New political planks rammed into your platforms against the wishes of the majority are without significance. The phrase, "The Solid South," which meant something vital at one time, has no meaning in these days of quick change and movie-show influences.

Democracy, in some sections, is a matter of climate. If you have come to a point where science and sentimentality are engaged in a drastic war, then the Democratic phalanx must undergo some rude changes.

The Democratic tail wagged the Republican dog for some time, but that curious spectacle has lost its hold on public interest. It is not now a question of one end wagging the other, but who will wag both. If Republicans stand for crude force, and Democrats for antebellum sentimentality, both are doomed together.

In the South, Democracy means politics at the polls, aristocracy in the parlor. In the North, Republicanism means the aristocracy of wealth.

However, your conception of social equality is undergoing modification.

In Washington's time the slogan was revolution; in Lincoln's time it was abolition; in your time it is prohibition, which reminds me that laws passed in haste bring long periods of repentance.

Effective effrontery is the result of courageous ignorance, for millions are more easily influenced by illusive promises than by the lessons of experience.

Modern civilization has hurried to meet four deadly things—riches, pleasures, materialism and war. But the tortoise is a better example of progress than the hare fleeing before the greyhound.

ELIZABETH CADY STANTON

It appalls the normal mind to stop and consider the criminal blunders made by the educated Prussian and the educated Englishman prior to 1914. No statesman had the vision to see what was going to happen to the man-made world.

Since it is a question of intuition and feeling versus cold reason and business logic, let us see which side is the more vital and all-enduring. Let us consider for a brief space what it is that influences people. Let us consider the influence exerted by the arts. What is music? Emotion created by sound vibrations. What is dramatic acting? Emotion created by vocal vibrations combined with gesture and physical movement. Has anyone ever witnessed automatic acting that left a profound impression?

Orators become famous when they unite deep feeling with knowledge. But what gives expression? The power of awakening emotion in others. Feeling is always more convincing than intellect. Intellect is full of theories, notions and superstitions. But where you find deep feeling combined with knowledge, you will find reason directed by qualities which pass through the surface and attain the heart-throbs of the real.

There are many kinds of emotion. There is the hard emotion of anger, the confused emotion of fear, the painful emotion of jealousy, the indescribable emotion of despair, the radiant emotion of joy. But the greatest emotion of all is that of knowledge united to feeling.

Men, as a rule, speak of emotion as a weakness, and they confuse it with impulse—a very different thing. Impulse is often the result of weak nerves, uncontrolled by the will; but we must not confuse it with the emotional quality which underlies all great achievement in art, literature, philosophy and personality. The more impulsive the individual is, the more primitive the reasoning faculty.

English and American business men are limited in general knowledge. I have never been able to discover any distinctive difference between the two. In France and Italy many business men are able to discuss art, literature and music on the same level with the masters. The Latin races and the Celtic races possess a culture that can be traced back for two or three thousand years, but Anglo-Saxon culture only to the time of the Saxon invasion. The Anglo-Saxons were the mushrooms of our civilization. They were a stolid business people who lacked creative genius.

The outstanding intellect of England today is Celtic. The Scotch, the Irish and the Welsh combine emotion and power with tenacity of purpose, and it is this Celtic element that keeps America in the front rank of nations.

What women have been opposing is the primitive monotony of the Anglo-Saxon trend. It has meant a mixture of politics and commerce so primitive and so naive that Frenchmen are amazed when they visit America and note the striking difference between the culture of the women and the mentality of the average man.

One of your great mystics has said: "The chemical constituents of human bodies is the same. The ashes of a saint and the ashes of a sinner give the same chemical results. As human bodies they are the same, but their functions separate them and make them totally different, so that the difference cannot by any hocus-pocus of metaphysics or magic be bridged or spanned."

Two things of the same material are really different if their functions are different. The real substance of a thing is in its function. We have to judge people by the things they do, not by their appearance; for there is no clear understanding between two persons whose aims are different. This is why there are so many divorces. This is why so many intellectual women live separate lives from their husbands in the same house.

People seem to be similar and equal but they differ according to their functions. If we take a philosopher, a hangman and a sailor who appear to be equal as human beings we shall see that in their functions there is nothing in common. The souls of these men are different in the very nature, origin and purpose of their existence.

Thousands of people move in a world of material shadows while their souls, the substance of which is intellectual and spiritual, inhabit a sphere absolutely apart. Especially is this the case with many of the cultured women of our time who are compelled to live a double life. Their intellects are far removed from the ordinary pursuits of the commercial world.

A woman of spiritual culture who marries a commercial man has married a shadow. A woman of high ideals who marries a professional politician has hitched her motor car to a meteor. A romantic woman married to a multi-millionaire whose world is bound in liberty bonds loses her liberty. A metaphysical woman who marries a financier is handicapped by the physical.

A union of spiritual functions with material formulas is impossible, for there is no way in which mere sensation can be made to harmonize with the higher emotions.

The new era of woman, which is just beginning to dawn, will direct education; and through education, politics; through politics, the progress of nations. Heretofore, the commercial and political world had a free hand. The progressive element was confined to a limited number of men in the colleges and the ministry, together with a remnant of law-makers. But their influence was negative owing to lack of material support.

Women will now present a formidable force in numbers, backed by a spiritual power, aided by men who understand the difference between functions and appearance, sensuous desires and ideal emotions.

For years I maintained that women do not realize the power they possess. They live so much in a world of their own that they do not regard the man-made commercial world as worth elevating.

Thousands of men are living in a sphere some degrees below the normal. They have been surrounded from the beginning with influences that obliterate all the higher faculties of the mind.

It has taken woman some centuries to rise to power, but the work is only half done. Never can the commercial instinct and the intellectual ideal be made to harmonize. The two spheres of consciousness are totally distinct.

The modern intellect has been organized without considering the moral meaning of its activity. This has caused the delusion that the crowning glory of European culture is the dreadnaught. Ninety per cent of all modern inventions are for bodily destruction or bodily comfort. While the body lolls in luxury, the spirit is soused in lethargy. As Ouspensky says, we have created two lives—one material, the other spiritual. I believe this is owing to the fact that man is living and working in the material and woman in the spiritual. In other words, she is carrying her own responsibilities on one shoulder and man's baneful burdens on the other. The figure of Atlas holding up the Globe should be changed to that of a female.

One would think that in these days, when psychology is taught even to children, that a man who has lived forty years in the world of action would know better than to boast of his eternal activities. The word "busy" has grown to be a veritable fetish with thousands who have little or nothing to do. The truth is, most men are not half as busy as they seem and not more than a fourth as wise as they look.

We have to find out by exact analysis just what incentive lies behind people's actions. What makes the distinction is the quality of our acts. Everything in the material and the spiritual worlds is judged according to quality. Gold, diamonds, clothes, bricks, music, poetry, literature, are adjudged, in the last resort, on the basis of intrinsic value. When people are engaged in pursuits for the sake of money the results will be on a plane with the quality of the incentive.

In the work done by women in the past fifty years in this country, the incentive has been of a higher quality than that shown by men.

While men introduced a coarse realism into the novel, women saved the situation by new ideals. I do not think there would be much left worth reading today but for woman's taste and judgment.

In the world of intellect and emotion things hang together. A low plane of intellect will produce low impulses. The more we know the greater our control of the different sense organs. Nothing can happen without a corresponding cause behind it.

The hysteria so common at great political conventions is caused by the exceedingly limited intelligence of the managers and directors who labor under the illusion that blind impulse is tantamount to vision. In other words, where the critical faculties are not developed anything can happen. And it is not difficult to predict that when political conventions are swayed by hysterical temperaments the authority at the White House will have all he can do to steer the Ship of State through the troubled waters of impulse and confusion.

There is a will to power that is blind. There is another will to power that brings the higher emotions to bear on the lower impulses, controls and directs the organs of sense.

The people who elect a President are the ones who will influence his actions. And when we talk about a President being a good man for business we are compelled to seek for the reason behind the statement.

If finance lands a President at the White House, women, children, teachers and philosophers must shift for themselves, since the supreme test lies in function, and not in manners, words and looks. And finance means finesse.

Do not expect great innovations at the Capitol until a strong woman takes her seat at the White House; and by this I do not mean one of Barnum's bearded ladies.

Conservatism is a good thing when it is coupled with vision and judgment, but bear in mind that monotony and mediocrity start in the same groove, run at the same pace and arrive at the same grave.

BENJAMIN FRANKLIN

There is but one mark of patriotism and that is vigilance and enthusiasm. The cause of your trouble is the sincerity with which your foes think and act and the lukewarm sentiment shown by Americans. The reason is to be found in the comfort and luxury of the present day compared with the pioneer sacrifices of your fathers and grandfathers. Your opponents are vindictive as well as vigilant. They mean what they say and do what they will. They are working as individuals, as well as in groups and parties, but Americans who inherited the land with liberty are exchanging both for the license of the maw.

When school teachers and farm hands are permitted to leave the country for the city, the end is not so far off as your sophisticated solons of the State Capitols would lead you to suppose.

I once stated that three movings equal one fire, and I can say now that the lack of teachers and farm hands has resulted in a damage equal to one revolution. No calamity comes and goes single handed. The world, the flesh and the devil are a triumvirate bound together by ties of consanguinity. Your school teachers are passing over to the world, your farm laborers to the flesh, and your ministers to the devil.

You are browsing on the stubble. One delinquency involves another, and eventually the monetary capital of the nation may be reduced to that of France. The nation will awake one day to the disillusioning fact that peace and progress cannot be gauged by commercial prosperity alone. For without food what avails your steel, your oil and your gold?

If you could witness the mortification poor Andrew Carnegie is now undergoing because of his lack of vision, you would have a lesson not soon forgotten. He built libraries but furnished no books to fill them. It was like building houses without windows. When leading business men commit such folly what can you expect of the nation at large?

The three things most needed by the people are food, raiment and shelter. The next three are instruction, religion and discipline. Liberty is a privilege; it comes after all the others. The individual has no rights inimical to those of the collective conscience.

Until you learn this fundamental maxim, all your knowledge will prove but a sounding brass and a tinkling cymbal.

The nations are rattling over the cobble stones of bankruptcy on a buckboard of compromise, on the high road to revolution.

JOHN MARSHALL
(The Expounder of the Constitution)
Recorded October, 1920

Some recent decisions of the Supreme Court of the United States are, more than any other factor, calculated to develop and foster an element of national unrest. Its deliberations are beyond the intelligence of many and above the interests of the majority. Its psychology is that of a divorce between capital and labor. Its rulings remind me of what transpired in England early in the nineteenth century.

Many who were not socialists are beginning to turn from the older order, imbued with the feeling that nothing could happen in the future worse for the country at large than the conditions that are being endured in the present.

A revolution arrives after a series of connected events which exhausts the patience of the public, and events are moving with intensity as well as rapidity.

DANIEL WEBSTER

You will search the pages of history in vain without finding a parallel to present conditions.

The war gave Bohemia her freedom; at the same time it licensed a bohemian poet to keep Italy stewing in her own juice, a bohemian journalist from New York to direct affairs in Moscow, and a bohemian socialist from Switzerland to rule over Russia.

Added to this a fashionable ladies' pianist has tried his hand, or should I say fingers, in the science of unfurling the sails of Poland's new Ship of State, while shop-keepers direct affairs in Germany and pusilanimous politicians keep the people of America in a state of tepid trepidation and flatulent turmoil. Can you wonder that the country is being hypnotized by the sight of so many cantankerous cataleptics? Macbeth declared he had waded in so far that returning would be as perilous as going on. Nothing will move them until they are swamped by the high tide of reaction and flung as flotsam on the rocks of a stormy opportunism.

A new Damocles has a sword suspended over the National Capitol, and liberty hangs to the hinges of the Constitution by a hair.

OLIVER WENDELL HOLMES

While a few people are ready to return to first principles, many are giving expressions to Garden of Eden proclivities. But instead of the old Eve, you have the new Amazon; instead of the old serpent, copperheads in Congress; instead of the old Adam, fresh brands of bluebeards.

Agreeable to the apple of the new Adam's eye and the fruitarian diet of the new Eden, some ladies have adopted the fig-leaf standard. But let that pass for the moment, always bearing in mind that he who loses his sense of humor loses his equilibrium.

Millions of people are dancing their legs off to keep their heads on.

Providence is wiser than the moralists.

There was a way out of the trenches and there is a way out of the pessimism developed by the dying dispensation. It is not so much a question of keeping your powder dry as it is of keeping your wits from congealing.

Beware of nebulous notions and theories. Uncanny kinks lead to calamitous brain storms. A stitch in the side saves nine—kicks behind the solar plexus.

BENJAMIN WADE
(Late Governor of Ohio—U. S. Senator)

Viewed in the light that shines on the White House, there is no difference between a man from Ohio and a gentleman from Indiana.

Men from the pumpkin pie districts think and feel alike, judging world politics by the yard-stick method that prevailed in their villages when they were young men. They are not always aware that political ruts cause social ructions.

The all-wool-and-a-yard-wide politician was home-spun and honestly patriotic, but what you need is a home-spun thinker whose vision has got beyond the yard-stick measure and can take in the whole world.

An old-school president, at this juncture, will have little more authority than a Congo king would have at a conference of jurists in Paris.

Has anyone taken the trouble to find out just what distinguishes the minority from the majority?

While the home-spun politician was eating cookies and buckwheat cakes made by his mother in the Middle West, some millions in New York, Chicago, Cleveland, and other foreign centers, were partaking of wienerwurst, sauerkraut, Swiss cheese and rye bread, and clinking beer glasses, according to the custom of Continental Europe.

If we say that a statesman represents Americanism, the question arises what kind of Americanism? The Yankee, the Southerner, each had his place in the political economy of America from 1776 to the Emancipation Proclamation in 1863, and even up to the Cleveland Administration, after which conditions began to change with startling rapidity, when the children born of foreign parents were beginning to come of age and the European ferment began to leaven the lumps of sectional dough.

The man who occupies the White House in 1921 should take Time by the forelock and the profiteer with the padlock, know how to translate "Es ist verboten" into Russian, and say, "Get thee behind me, Satan," in Esperanto.

If honesty, alone, is the best and only policy, our country would be safe, but honesty is only one of the qualities necessary in these days to carry a President through the mazes of a complex administration. Honesty does not always imply clear vision or even ordinary common sense. The faculties of diplomatic tact and political judgment are infinitely more important, and experience still more so.

In America the roles enacted by professional politicians remind one of a masquerade where everyone is trying to penetrate behind the masks and guessing is the rule. If in this heterogeneous ball-room you slap your partner on the back, you may elicit a grunt from a grouchy bolshevik or a groan from a disgruntled "bohemian."

And yet Congress enacts laws for Americans who understand no dialect but their own and who have to engage interpreters when they visit Paris. How many wealthy Americans realize that these United States have outgrown the cookie era, the buckwheat pancake era, the corn cob era, the wooden nutmeg era, and arrived at the root-hog-or-die era?

Young America today no more resembles the young America of thirty years ago than a butterfly resembles a caterpillar. Young men and women are sixty per cent cosmopolitan and forty per cent rebel. During the next five years the number of young people who will insist on thinking for themselves will increase two-fold, because in that time many thousands of children born of foreign parents in America will have become mature enough to have fixed upon some sort of ideal.

Congress will realize the situation when it is too late for regrets to be of any service. Which calls to mind a story apropos of this pressing subject: A landlady, having no means of obtaining meat for her boarders, made a stew out of a litter of kittens. The truth became known in a day or two. One of the boarders said the very thought made her sick, to which the landlady replied: "Feeling sick won't do no good; them kittens has all been digested."

DON PIATT
(Late Editor of "The Capital," Washington, D. C.)

Where are the debaters whose rapier tongues ripped up the rag dolls of Congress and kept the floor of the House supplied with fresh sawdust, whose fantastic fencing and heart-piercing thrusts were the delight of the gallery and the terror of fire eaters. Gone, gone where the woodbine twineth. What went they out for to see? A reed shaken by the wind? There is a difference in reeds. Tom Reed of Maine shook the House, but the House never shook him. What were his favorite drinks? There was plenty to choose from in the Washington of his day. But note the difference between the wit of the Maine Reed and that of the Missouri Reed.

On the other hand, where did Bryan get the "cross of gold" inspiration in the old days? Did he do it on tannic acid released from tea leaves? Who will ever know? One thing is certain—he never again rose to the same level.

Is our planet revolving toward a second edition of puritanism? Probably. The esprit de corps that animated the body politic begins to resemble a corpse with the esprit evaporated.

The human mind needs moments of exaltation as well as relaxation. Brilliant results are not produced by lukewarm sentiments expressed in a voice that lacks enthusiasm.

Washington is now a resort for celluloid cynics and a refuge for asbestos patriots whose marmorian snobbery makes me think of the ruins of temples abandoned by the gods and forgotten by man.

The great blunder of the prohibitionists was made when they condemned beer and light wine. Nature abhors abruptness. Progress is not made by sudden jerks and violent laws passed in a hurry.

If a few persons living in an obscure village in Ohio can bring about a movement like prohibition, the same influence can bring about a return of the old Connecticut blue laws.

Violent actions are followed by violent reactions. From this there is no escape.

The fundamental objection to prohibition, as it stands, lies in the cold fact that provincialism, no matter how sincere, can never compete with international common sense and cosmopolitan culture.

Village residents are ignorant of the laws that govern society in the most intelligent centers of the world. What will be the result in the long run? Antagonism between the people of the cities and the people of the country.

When they prohibit tobacco, a war of cuss words will be followed by a battle of cuspidors, and the very crows will cuss the crocuses.

BENJAMIN DISRAELI

Some Members of Parliament have lost their reason, the majority have lost their wits, all are without vision.

Lloyd George presents the curious spectacle of a man of the people who observes them through the glasses of a Welsh Calvinist. He is a democrat with the demeanor of a lord, a radical who has fallen between the two stools of the middle-class and the landed aristocracy. Nonconformist sentimentality, on one hand, and titled wealth on the other, have blinded him to the imperative needs of the time and the dangers that confront the Empire.

The English people of the past twenty years have suffered as much from misgovernment as the Germans and the Russians, but they cannot stop the present stream of progress by clatter in the House and appeals to patriotism.

For years England has been saddled with cabinets composed of professional humorists and hum-drum moralists.

Augustine Birrell was a diluted edition of Sydney Smith, and Bonar Law should have been a professor of theology in a Presbyterian seminary. Sir Edward Carson played the role of an unfrocked priest in the service of demiurgos. Earl Curzon is a political derelict whose presence in the Council Chamber prevents unity and impedes progress.

History will record their acts as the most amazing in the annals of Great Britain. I see nothing for the old order but unconditional surrender. The hand-writing on the wall was visible in 1909, but no preparation was made for the change which is now sweeping the country with cyclonic force.

We, from our side, can do no more than utter some words of warning for the few who have ears to hear, the tidal wave of change not being confined to particular countries or regions.

I, too, when Prime Minister, was blind to the reality, having been born and reared in an atmosphere as foreign to that of the masses as the atmosphere of the Winter Palace was foreign to the peasants of Russia.

We staggered under the load of a wealthy and titled upper class. They consumed the people's time and imposed infinite misery on some millions of toilers, and for these things we rewarded the men at the top with fresh titles.

As you know, I led the Conservative Party in England for many years, but that Party was, and still is, avid for power.

The Liberal Party was made up of men using Nonconformity as an instrument of advancement. They placed opportunity above the truth, position above principle, power above progress. We were all intellectual automatons, set in motion by springs wound up by leaders who were themselves automatons.

England goes by machinery. Her very existence is mechanical. Now, when a loose screw stops the evolution of the wheels, the whole nation stops.

In what way can we be said to excel in probity of conduct the people of Ireland? In what way are we superior to Irish politicians? The scandals that occurred in London during the war would not have been tolerated in Dublin under an Irish Parliament. And still England is being led by a Welsh Calvinist, opposed by a Scottish humorist who says his prayers, backed by Anglican agnostics and middle-class dissenters overwhelmed with fear.

We always imitate the French, but while we accepted Voltairianism in principle, the French had the courage to put it into practice. While the French became practical pagans in 1789, we became practical hypocrites.

It is this element that has created the moral indifference of the Anglican Church and the intellectual apathy of the so-called Nonconformist conscience. This is why there is no stability behind the old phraseology, the old ceremonials, the old confessions of faith—now so many catch-words which the people abhor. And this is why the working men find it so easy to send their leaders to Parliament. For the same reason Russian radicalism is certain of a warm welcome on English soil.

It is true that this hypocrisy is subconscious, having had its origin during the French Revolution. This renders it far more dangerous because political leaders in England today are mentally incompetent to realize the danger that lies before them.

We cannot reason with people whose vision is dulled by four generations of moral apathy. Hence they will continue to "kick against the pricks" to the bitter end. There will be strife added to strife, confusion to confusion, and they, themselves, will invite the drastic events which must follow so much stubborn resistance to the demands of common justice and the progress of civilization.

PRINCE BISMARCK
Recorded November 3d, 1920

When I imposed an indemnity of five billion francs on the French people in 1870 we knew that the money could and would be paid. But there is no parallel between Germany in 1920 and France in 1870. The Reparations Commission has only succeeded in proving its incompetence. The German delegates have shown that the Allied war claims amount to more than five hundred billion marks (gold), which is nearly four thousand billions at the present rate of exchange. This fantastic sum, one hundred times more than France paid to Germany in 1870, is expected of a country on the verge of revolution and chaos. I charge this Commission with incompetence, extravagance, luxurious living, and claims at once absurd and ridiculous.

You punish some of the most dangerous criminals by indeterminate sentences, which frequently end after a year's imprisonment, but you expect to hold the German people in financial bondage for more than a generation to come because of the criminal blunders of less than a hundred individuals.

I was blinded by material factors at the time of my seeming triumphs but now I can see some of the things which will never come to pass. The French and the English are repeating some of the blunders I made fifty years ago. They are counting on conditions which will never exist, like a bird sitting on a nest of mixed eggs from which the cuckoo will eventually oust all the other birds.

French people are under the illusion that Russia will meet the obligations undertaken by the late Czar. To expect such a thing shows the child-like illusions under which French fanatics are living. They are still wrapped in the swaddling clothes of politics.

We committed crimes that have brought civilization to the brink of chaos, but we are not capable of such naivete.

The logic of a Frenchman is no better than the mysticism of a Russian or the sentimentality of an Englishman. French people learned nothing from the blunders of Napoleon III and the debacle of Sedan. And the reason? They have remained provincial while the Germans imitated the commercial cosmopolitanism of the English.

Advice is the cheapest of all things. Nevertheless, I advise your statesmen to place no reliance on sentimental contracts written on paper foredoomed to become "scraps."

I do not hesitate to declare that no agreement signed since 1913 is worth more than the seals. In Europe, leaders and rulers have passed from an international game of chess to a national gamble with marked cards.

You have now to deal with an element which did not exist in my time. This element embraces all factions of the new radicalism, no matter in what country or under what leader. Some of these elements may unite, but they are not going to change. How, then, can you undertake to insure the future by contracts signed and sealed by elderly gentlemen with good intentions and poor judgment?

The war gave the new factions the long wished-for opportunity. They seized it in Russia, in Germany, in Poland, in Britain, and other countries. But the opportunities created by the war are one thing, the opportunities of tomorrow will be different, and it is this contingency for which your leaders are not prepared. You will have to select men of vision who will judge events as they arrive, without regard to the distant future, which belongs to no man.

One of my greatest mistakes was in separating Protestant Prussia from the interests of the Catholics of South Germany.

The new radicalism is opposed to some things which are irrevocably linked with religious doctrine.

Without the Catholic Church all Europe would be in the throes of the Commune. The principal cause of our disintegration was that we sanctioned Protestant flirtation with modern materialism.

France is beginning to see that even a weak monarchy is better than a radical government without a God.

You may expect a return of the monarchy in more than one country. Agnostics and Protestants, moved by fear on one side, and disgust on the other, will unite for a restoration as their last hope. There will be a repetition of historic events.

Bonaparte was ushered in by the French Revolution, and his advent was followed by three kings and one emperor.

The majority treat their rulers as children treat their toys: when the novelty wears off a change is demanded.

Political psychology and religious sentiment are not the same thing. Nevertheless, they must be considered together. The Germans are now awaiting the hour when the inevitable change will be demanded. Events take crowns from some heads and place them on others. If the ex-Kaiser ever occupies the throne again a modern Nero will fiddle amidst the ruins of German imperialism, for you know he meddled with fiddle strings as well as with political wires.

You think it strange? The impossible is always happening. Never lose sight of the fact that an organized minority is more formidable than a disorganized majority. Three men brought about the coup d'etat that placed the outcast Louis Napoleon on the throne, one man started the Russian Revolution, I planned the overthrow of the Second Empire with the aid of Count von Moltke. The majority put their trust in numbers, but the bigger a thing grows the nearer it is to disintegration. An autocratic minority ruled in Germany, an automatic majority rules in France and England. Two men started the present rule in Moscow, both of them from the outside.

"God has been merciful to us," said Cavour, in the Italian Senate, "He has made Spain one degree lower than Italy." God has been merciful to Germany, He has made Russian communism more abhorrent than German socialism.

Nothing will be left undone by the French government to secure permanent occupation of the coal district of the Rhine.

Conditions will not remain long as they are. They are preparing decisive coups in Bavaria, Hanover, Austria and Hungary. New combinations will amaze your statesmen and diplomats, who are ignorant of the fact that changes and upheavals operate in cycles of three and seven. What they call chance is the working of law. Spiritual forces operate through the physical, and nature will take a hand in the reactions in Petrograd and Moscow. Cold, hunger and starvation will dissipate the hopes of the ruling minority. Untold numbers will be sacrificed.

During the French Revolution philosophers and thinkers were decapitated. In Russia such men are killed by hunger, the difference being one of method.

Such conditions will be repeated in different countries until people learn that the spiritual cannot be separated from the material without pain and slaughter.

After all the long-winded conferences and shorthand reports nothing is left but a confusion of blots on the tissue paper of time.

I may say more on another occasion.

HENRY WARD BEECHER

The happy-go-lucky humor of the day is no match for the cool calculation of European communists. English and American humorists do for the public what the court jester once did for blasé kings. In the sardonic temper of the Russian revolutionist, I see a return of the French temper of 1793. Most of the sermons and speeches of the time are chameleon in character and tepid in feeling. English humorists developed a flagrant cynicism, spotted with a varioloid paradox, while French writers have halted between the isolation of the hospital and the insularity of the home.

The war brought Anatole France to his senses, the last of the Gallic wits, who possessed a greater charm than Voltaire without attaining his universal prestige. Prince Bismarck declares that the French have learned nothing since their defeat at Sedan. Yet French writers have learned more from the great war than the writers of any other country.

English humor is meant to entertain a public lost in the cynical buffooneries of materialism; American humor is meant to amuse a public lost in the mazes of extravagant pleasures and provincial inanities.

English humor has a certain seal; American humor a certain mark—the difference between sealing wax and a postage stamp. Both aim to fill the ghastly gap left by the doctrine of evolution since it caught the fancy of agnostic freebooters in 1870—forerunners of

something grimmer than the Soviet symbols of a return of puritanism even now creeping into view as ivy creeps up the water spouts.
Laughter will vanish, since there will be nothing left to laugh at. Dancing will cease, for curfew will ring at nine and people will begin work at five.

Remember that all the great modern movements had an obscure origin. Spiritualism began in a country farm-house, Christian Science developed out of mediumship, prohibition was started in a village, woman's suffrage was started by a Quakeress, Theosophy began at a farm-house in Vermont, the Salvation Army was started by a group of obscure persons.

The new puritanism will start by a committee of persons unknown to the public, chosen from the ranks of the Methodists, Baptists and Presbyterians. Grim determinists, they will ignore satire, sarcasm and irony, ignore party politics, ignore the opposition of luke-warm Christians, form committees, in which they will be aided by drastic reactions during the period of readjustment.

Centers will soon be formed in Atlanta, Nashville, Cleveland, Boston, Hartford, Philadelphia and Washington, D. C.

What is causing so much crime? Not one, but many elements of decadence, all operating together, among which I can name rag, jazz, high balls, cabarets, free verse, neurotic art, sentimental optimism, cheap notions of progress, neutral sermons, automobilism, lack of child discipline, absence of fear among people under the age of forty—evils which you may apply to all English-speaking countries.

The licence of the cities dominates country life and country thought. The city minority rules the majority in the country, and it is in the country that the reaction will begin.

JOHN MARSHALL
(Second Message)

Many of the smaller nations, instead of being content with their liberty, have thrown it away for the licence that always goes with land grabbing. For a nation is nothing more than an individual with a certain amount of collective ambition.

Much of the work of the League of Nations will have to be undone. But it will not be undone by any League. The nations will settle differences in accordance with the law that permits the more powerful to wield control commensurate with their geographical and intellectual importance.

All people have rights which ought to be respected, but some have privileges as well as rights, and the privileged will hold the upper hand as long as intelligence takes precedence of illiteracy, energy dominates over lethargy, and the power of organized numbers rules over minorities.

Your statesmen and your mediators will have to learn the distinction between rights and privileges. All are supposed to possess common rights under the common law, but it is wisdom, supported by poise and power, that constitutes privilege. David and Solomon were privleged. So were Alfred the Great, Washington and Lincoln.

A nation is temperamental like an individual. The temperament may be vascillating or it may be stolid; it may be logical or it may be commercial; or a combination of the Saxon and the Celt.

The nations that will hold the balance of power in the future will be the ones with the most will and poise, backed by number. Riches, alone, will not save. Wealth did not save Germany from disaster, nor did it help Napoleon III to ward off the Prussian invasion in 1870. Wealth invites invasion and conquest. This is why England and America will now be the principal target for the ambitious and the discontented. This is why Japan seeks a firm foothold in China, and the Russians an entrance to India through Persia.

Without the prospects of loot there would be no war. When ambition and glory lure a nation on, the desire for loot supplies the motor force. When hunger forces a people to invade a nation, loot becomes a necessity.

What the wealthy of every nation refuse to understand, or even to consider, is that material force engenders vanity, individualism, rivalry and envy. All manifestations of force contain an element of disintegration. The type of a nation will always represent the policy and the trend of the nation.

The supreme blunder of the Peace Conference was made when the delegates, with Mr. Wilson at their head, refused to face the fact that no nation can rise above the ideals and idiosyncrasies of the national temperament, and that sudden liberation from restraint is as dangerous for a country as it is for an individual.

There is but one step between liberty and licence, and that step meant pandemonium for all classes in Russia. For other peoples it may mean political bondage and the total loss of a national spirit. For the Hindoos it will mean civil wars between the different native rulers, for China it has meant a series of revolutions and counter revolutions which may have to be suppressed by the drastic hand of a Japanese Bonaparte.

The League Conference at Versailles took no account of the working of natural law. Sentimentality was the key-note of Mr. Wilson's idealism, and commercial expansion the dominant idea of his opponents.

As for religion exerting any fundamental influence for peace and right thinking, it caused Protestants to fight Protestants and Catholics to fight Catholics, while German and Austrian cardinals did all in their power to aid in the invasion and conquest of Belgium and France, on one hand, and Italy, the stronghold of the Papal See, on the other; and all this in the face of the statement of the Kaiser that Catholicism must be destroyed. Nothing like it has been known since the dawn of Christianity.

The only apparent reason for the quiescent attitude of some of the smaller nations is that they are without the material means of waging war on their neighbors.

Just as long as politicians are impelled by self-interest there will be found nations that will have to use force for the suppression of licence and the curtailment of liberty. In every country the people are getting what their thoughts and deeds create for them.

ABRAHAM LINCOLN

Events come and go in cycles—there is a beginning, a middle and an end. The League of Nations had a beginning and it will have an end. But what kind of an end? Will it be one of victory or one of ignominy?

The two fatal blunders of the Kaiser and his cohorts consisted in the delusion that England could not raise, equip and transport a body of troops sufficient to offer adequate resistance to the invaders of France in conjunction with the French and Belgian armies, and that America could not or would not join the European Allies.

At the present juncture the inimical forces, both in continental Europe and in America, are repeating the old blunders under fresh conditions.

History is a repetition of the old tunes with new variations. Just now the fireworks of sophistry and rhetoric drown out the familiar tune and what is heard is the buzz-saw of political machinery.

Hyenas are gnawing the bones left by the lion rampant of Czardom; and Siberia, the remnant, is being consumed by jackals from Japan. It remains to be seen how long voters with American pedigrees will be influenced by demagogues who would induce them to part with their birthright for a mess of pottage burnt on the bottom.

The longer you wink at anarchy in Europe the greater will be the menace of social chaos at home. The worship of shibboleths cannot be kept up beyond a point where the majority grow tired of hocus-pocus politics and academical agnosticism.

PSYCHO-PHONE MESSAGES 57

There should be harmony of interests in dealing with the people of Mexico, from whom you have much to learn in many ways.

The Obregon Government should be recognized at Washington and immediate steps taken to insure cordial relations between the two countries.

The City of Mexico is a capital with a great future.

You are about to pass through a period of great confusion. Warnings have been given but not heeded. Unless you cease to theorize, and propagate a spirit of justice and judgment, the near future will develop something more than storms in the blue china teapots of diplomacy.

ROBERT G. INGERSOLL

Washington needs a breaker of images.

The pedestrian sauntering down Pennsylvania Avenue cannot but note the hefty Hancock on horseback, looking as if he had just left a meeting of ward politicians, and, in another part of the city, McClellan, the Beau Brummel of the Civil War, on a charger, sniffing the smoke of battle from a safe distance, and others whose names are writ in water but whose effigies remain in bronze.

To the scrap heap with these, and in their places erect memorials for the women, who did as much for America as Joan of Arc did for France, the intrepid pioneers of their race, the prophetic patriots of the nineteenth century—Elizabeth Cady Stanton, Lucretia Mott and Susan B. Anthony.

It would take a Lincoln Memorial to depict their serenity, a National Capitol to symbolize their nobility, a Washington Monument to typify the towering height of their achievement and the scope and clarity of their vision.

STEPHEN A. DOUGLAS

A war between America and England would fill your homes with desolation and bring ruin to the whole country. Do your sins of omission merit such a punishment? I am here to tell you what to expect if such a hurricane of disaster ever sweeps the two countries.

Millions of people are under the impression that the United States can act independently of the conditions prevailing in the other great nations. This suggestion, coming, as it did, from a professional joker in England, has met with eager response from revolutionary emissaries now in your midst, supported by political fillibusters who are masking the truth.

If England ever starts such a war she will lose India. Her direction of the reins of civilization in many quarters of the world would cease on the day hostilities began. But I am speaking for America.

A war with England would Russianize the United States within three months. Even if the navy could keep the enemy at a safe distance the destructive forces at home would loot the principal cities and spread terror from ocean to ocean.

The first to lose in such an upheaval would be the wealthy propagandists of disorder and violence, who, living in security now, would be hurled with destructive force against the weapons of their own creation.

GENERAL BENJAMIN H. GRIERSON
Late Commander of the Military Department of
Southern California, Arizona and New Mexico

In 1914 western civilization was threatened by a military autocracy centralized at Berlin. Europe is now threatened by a communistic tyranny centralized at Moscow and by an autocratic aristocracy centered in Japan, anti-Christian, anti-democratic, anti-American. You may call it fate or destiny, it matters not so long as you know what the signs and portents are.

We can see what is going on in the navy yards of the Nipponese Empire. We have noted the strenuous efforts put forth in naval preparations there.

A Japanese Bonaparte will soon dominate China and prevent Christian propaganda throughout Asia. I could give you the dates fixed for certain maneuvers and events in connection with Japanese ambitions relating to America, but they could change the dates. Suffice it to say they are making ready as fast as possible, much faster than many in this country could be made to believe. When the decisive moment arrives for action it will come suddenly, like the invasion of Belgium by the Germans.

Here are some of their expectations:—

The invasion of the coast of Mexico and a coalition of Japanese forces with some military faction in Mexico likely to be of practical aid, the bombing of American cities on the Pacific Coast from the air, virtual cessation of communication between certain sections east of the Rocky Mountains and California, brought about not so much by physical means as by revolutionary influences. They are counting on a Soviet revolution east of the Rockies while they are gaining a foothold in California.

One of their first attempts would be to bomb the railway passes in the Cascades and the Sierra Nevadas.

General Grant has warned you in regard to the Panama Canal and other points that need immediate attention. Millions would be alarmed if they could realize how much the Government at Washington resembles the British Government just before the German descent into Belgium. Are they waiting until they can spy the enemy through field glasses?

I could give a map of the plans of approach of the Japanese navy, intended to operate in separate units, but it would do no good. They are ready to change their tactics at any time, and have done so more than once.

Let me add that the bellicose attitude of the war party in Japan is such that a war between England and America would be hailed as a symbol of their divine destiny.

Do not be surprised when I say that they proclaim the end of Christian civilization was reached when the Anglo-Saxons took possession of the Pacific Coast.

In the Far East, British domination attained its zenith in India; in America, Anglo-Saxon influence attained its limit in California. The possession of the Pacific Coast of North America is, therefore, the limit for the dominant white race. The tocsin has sounded for a Japanese avatar who will unify the political, commercial and religious forces of Japan and China, give the coup de grace to a tottering civilization and dominate the world. So do they reason and preach.

ALEXANDER HAMILTON

What do the clouds on the social horizon predict? Is Nature a book of fate? If so, is it sealed or open? Whoever understands the political actions of the past can foresee the reactions of the future.

Human nature is always the same.

The two things brought to the surface by great upheavals are extreme virtues and extreme vices. The virtue of self sacrifice, on the one hand, the vice of self interest on the other. Vice is flexible, cunning, adaptable.

You are living at a time when profiteers amaze by their cynical audacity, but profiteers have always existed. Before the war the nobles of Russia and Germany were profiteers in landed privileges and governmental perquisites. The tillers of the soil were free in name, serfs in practice. In England two or three hundred lords and peers possess the land. In America food profiteering began during the Civil War. This national vice has never been attacked at the roots.

Your age is characterized by a high level of predatory ability and a low level of prophetic visibility.

The old hackneyed phrase, "This is a free country," has been applied in varying degrees according to the caprice of the individual with the most aggressive will.

New words, definitions, excuses, have been invented to meet the new conditions, but of all the words yet brought into use, "camouflage" is the only one that covers the cynical effrontery of predatory hypocrisy. It is a vocable of universal utility. It applies to the cock-pits of commerce as well as to the arena of bull and bear politics.

It depicts a Hindoo patience in the pulpit and a Hoodoo palsy in the pews.

The word "democracy" itself is the stripes painted on the sides of the old Ship of State in her zig-zag course to elude the torpedoes of the proletarian submarines.

A capitalistic profiteer is a high brow optimist who lives by the sweat of the low brow pessimist. The stretching process will cease suddenly like the snapping of a rubber string stretched beyond the limit.

The masses without a voice always find articulation in the unlooked-for man, the unlooked-for group.

The people without a mouthpiece are a mob, and no mob can run itself for more than a few days. It is the initiated who lead, and leadership requires time, patience, judgment.

In the world of genius there are no upstarts.

The great leader never rises suddenly. Bonaparte was a military graduate, Grant was a product of West Point, Lincoln was thirty years preparing for the Presidency, Lenine spent twenty years in the study of economics. All countries have the same experience.

Voltaire endowed the middle classes of France with a voice, united the disaffected of all classes, and peppered their indignation with pungent epigrams. He created an intellectual garden for lovers of liberty, and from the realm of the mind flung the thorns of ridicule in the face of titled imbeciles and crowned the heads of scholars with laurel.

The people of France were washed by Louis XIV, wrung by Louis XV, and dried in the back yard of tyrannical economics by Louis XVI.

But it was the orators and pamphleteers who ironed out the frills and furbelows of the old order.

Statistical facts may convince but they do not compel. Who knows how the French Revolution would have ended had Mirabeau, orator of the great and solemn days, survived to put into action the idealism of Rousseau? Intellect alone never passes the halfway house. When intellect, reason and emotion are fused in one, the summit of achievement is attained.

PHILLIPS BROOKS

The time for discipline is approaching. Happy are those who, under Divine direction, consent to be led, for, in the words of Quintilian:—Nulla poena est nisi invito, or as Seneca expressed it, Fata volentum ducunt, involentem trahunt,—those who refuse will be dragged.

You must in some manner experience the ordeals common to other peoples, and you have seen from a distance what has overtaken many cities and nations, the inhabitants of which felt themselves as fixed as the rocks in the soil. Yet, all that is happening is in harmony with Divine law. You will find it in Isaiah and Jeremiah. The repetition is inevitable except for those who possess vision.

The time for appeals is past.

"The earth mourneth and fadeth away, the world languisheth and fadeth, the haughty people of the world do languish."

"When thou shalt cease to spoil, thou shalt be spoiled, and when thou shalt make an end to deal treacherously, they shall deal treacherously with thee."

Are the people astonished? Let them marvel at their own willfulness.

"The kings of the earth and all the inhabitants of the world would not have believed that the adversary and the enemy should have entered into the gates of Jerusalem."

Titus, with his army, destroyed the Holy City. The enemy entered the gates from without but your adversaries have long been entrenched within.

Mammon is heavily laden and will fall from the top. Material power is volatile.

In the day of trial, the retainer and the hireling will seek a refuge, every man for himself. They will melt like the wax image before the heat of the furnace. On that day humility will be as a precious gift and poverty as a peace offering.

Blessed is he who uses the spade and the hoe, for by the sweat of his brow he shall eat the bread of security.

www.ingramcontent.com/pod-product-compliance
Lightning Source LLC
Chambersburg PA
CBHW020628300426
44112CB00010B/1233